To

Gwen

From

Doris Jane

Chicken Soup for the Christian Soul™

Published by Blessings Unlimited
Pentagon Towers, P.O. Box 398004
Edina, MN 55439

Design by Lecy Design

ISBN 1-58375-613-2

A Little Spoonful of

Chicken Soup for the Christian Soul™

Golden Shoes
for Jesus

It was only four days before Christmas. The spirit of the season had not yet caught up with me, even though cars packed the parking lot of our local discount store. Inside the store, it was worse. Shopping carts and last-minute shoppers jammed the aisles.

Why did I come to town today? I wondered. My feet ached almost as much as my head. My list contained names of several people who claimed they wanted nothing, but I knew their feelings would be hurt if I didn't buy them something.

Buying for someone who had everything and deploring the high cost of items, I considered gift buying anything but fun.

Hurriedly, I filled my shopping cart with last-minute items and proceeded to the long checkout lines. I picked the shortest, but it looked as if it would mean at least a 20-minute wait.

In front of me were two small children—a boy of about five and a slightly younger girl. The boy wore a ragged coat. Enormously large, tattered tennis shoes jutted far out in front of his much-too-short jeans. He clutched several clumped dollar bills in his grimy hands.

The girl's clothing resembled her brother's. Her head was a matted mass of curly hair. Reminders of an evening meal showed on her small face. She carried a beautiful pair of shiny, gold house slippers. As the Christmas music sounded in the store's stereo system, the small girl hummed along, off-key, but happily.

When we finally approached the checkout register, the girl carefully placed the shoes on the counter. She treated them as though they were a treasure.

The clerk rang up the bill. "That'll be $6.09," she said.

The boy laid his crumpled bills atop the stand while he searched his pockets. He finally came up with $3.12. "I guess we'll have to put them back," he bravely announced.

With that statement, a soft sob broke from the little girl. "But Jesus would have loved these shoes," she cried.

"Well, we'll go home and work some more. Don't cry. We'll come back," the boy assured her.

Quickly I handed $3.00 to the clerk. These children had waited in line for a long time. And, after all, it was Christmas.

Suddenly a pair of arms came around me and a small voice said, "Thank you, lady."

"What did you mean when you said Jesus would like the shoes?" I asked.

The boy answered, "Our mommy is sick and going to heaven. Daddy said she might go before Christmas to be with Jesus."

The girl spoke. "My Sunday

school teacher said the streets up in heaven are shiny gold, just like these shoes. Won't my mommy be beautiful walking on those streets to match these shoes?"

My eyes flooded as I looked into her tear-streaked face. "Yes," I answered, "I'm sure she will."

Silently, I thanked God for

using these children to remind me of

the true spirit of giving.

HELGA SCHMIDT

I asked God for strength,

that I might achieve,

I was made weak, that I might

learn humbly to obey.

I asked for health, that I might

do greater things,

I was given infirmity,

that I might do better things.

I asked for riches,
that I might be happy,
I was given poverty,
that I might be wise.
I asked for power, that I might
have the praise of men,
I was given weakness,
that I might feel the need of God.

I asked for all things,

that I might enjoy life,

I was given life, that I might

enjoy all things.

I got nothing I asked for—

but everything I had hoped for.

Almost despite myself, my

unspoken prayers were answered.

I am, among all men,

most richly blessed.

Anonymous Confederate Soldier

In Jesus' Eyes

We wanted our son to know always that he was adopted. So from the time he was very young, we explained it to him in a way that was simple for him to understand.

"We were told that I could not have a baby in my belly and Jesus knew this," I said. "Jesus also knew that there was a lady who had a baby in her belly, but she could not be a mommy. From Heaven, Jesus saw this baby on the day he was born. Remembering that we wanted to be a mommy and daddy and that the lady could not be a mommy, Jesus decided that the baby belonged with us. That's how we became a family."

One day on our way home from the nursery school, our son asked me if he was born in Jesus' belly. I told him that he was not and once again we talked about how we became a family. After driving a little bit further I asked him if he had any questions.

He said, "Oh no, now I remember. I wasn't born in Jesus' belly, I was born in his eyes!"

HELEN MONTONE

Safety
Blanket

When I was fresh out of the seminary, my wife, Kathy, and I moved with our two-year-old son, Nate, to a small native village in Alaska. The small three- and four-passenger planes we took on our connecting flights so terrified our little boy that he took his favorite blanket and covered his head until we set down on the small dirt landing strips. Later, during the long adjustment months that followed, when we were learning how to live in a new place among new people of a different culture, my son carried his security blanket everywhere, and it soon became soft and well-worn. He couldn't fall asleep until he had his blanket and could snuggle into its warmth.

The second year that we were in the village, I had a chance to guest speak at a mission conference in Seattle. While I was packing for the trip, my son followed me around the room, asking where I was going, and how long would I be gone, and why did I have to speak to those people, and was anyone going with me? Fine-tuning my speech in my mind, I was a little distracted and concerned about catching the small plane out of the village on time. My son seemed most worried about my having to fly out in bad weather on one of those small planes he feared so much. I reassured him that I would be fine, and I asked him to take care of his mom until I came back. With a hug at the door, I was off to the village landing strip and on to my speaking engagement.

When I got to the hotel in Seattle, I didn't have time to unpack until later that evening, and I was horrified when I opened my luggage and found my son's security blanket inside. I pictured my wife trying desperately to find the lost blanket as she prepared our son for bed. I immediately rushed to the phone to call Kathy and tell her that the blanket was in my luggage, so she could reassure our frantic son.

Kathy picked up the phone and barely had time to answer when I began to explain that the blanket was in my luggage and I had no idea how it had accidentally been packed. I was in the midst of my apology when Kathy calmed me down with the news that she already knew where the blanket was.

She told me that she had picked Nate up and held him by the window to let him watch me drive away from the house. She had suggested that they pray for "Daddy to have a safe trip." Knowing that our son would be most afraid of the small plane ride to the major airport, she prayed, "Dear Lord, please help Daddy feel safe on the little plane." When the prayer was over, our son Nate spoke up and comforted his mom. "Don't worry,

Mom, I gave Daddy my blanket to

keep him safe."

REVEREND DR. BRUCE HUMPHREY

Give what you have.

To some one, it may be better

than you dare to think.

HENRY WADSWORTH LONGFELLOW

Helen's
Story

Helen Packer was 17 years old when I met her. A devout Christian and much-loved child, she was entering the hospital for the last time. Her diagnosis was lymphoma and all attempts at remission had failed. Helen shared with me, her nurse, that she could handle everything but the thought of dying alone.

She just wanted a loved one near her to hold her hand and pray with her. Helen's mother would stay at her bedside from early morning to late evening, return home for rest and resume the vigil come morning. Her father traveled in his job but relieved his wife as often as he could.

All of the nurses on the unit realized that Helen was precariously near death, as did she and her family. She began having seizures and lapses of consciousness.

As I was leaving the hospital at 11:00 one night, I noticed Helen's mother heading toward the parking garage as well. Our conversation was interrupted by the loudspeaker. "Outside call, Helen Packer. Please call the operator!"

Mrs. Packer reacted immediately with alarm. "Everyone knows how ill she is!" she blurted. "I'm going back to her room and see who is calling." With that she left me and returned to Helen. The operator reported that the calling party had hung up but left a message: "Tell Helen her ride will be late but is coming."

Baffled, Mrs. Packer stayed at Helen's bedside in anticipation of a mysterious visitor. Helen died at 1:13 a.m. with her mother at her side, holding her hand and praying.

When queried the next day, the operator couldn't remember even the gender of the caller. No other Helen Packer was found, employee or patient or visitor. For those of us who cared for, nurtured and prayed for Helen, there was only one answer.

Sandy Beauchamp

Give, and it will be given to you. A good measure, pressed down, shaken together and running over, will be poured into your lap.

LUKE 6:38 NIV

The Beautiful Color of Love

What color is God,
Asked the child with skin so fair
Is He white like me,
Does He have light hair

Is God dark like me,
Asked the child with skin of golden hue
Has He hair that's dark and curly,
Are His eyes black or blue

I think God is red like me,
The Indian boy is heard to say

He wears a crown of feathers,
And turns our nights to day

Each one of us knows that God is there,
In all the colors above
But be sure of this, the one color He is,
Is the beautiful color of love

So when your soul goes to Heaven,
When your life comes to its end
He will be waiting, and His hand to you
Will He extend.

There will be no colors in Heaven,
Everyone will be the same.
You will only be judged
by your earthly deeds,
Not your color or your name

So when your time comes,
And you see God in His Heaven above,
Then you will see the only color
that counts,
The beautiful color of love.

ARNOLD (SPARKY) WATTS

Faith

The fields were parched and brown from lack of rain, and the crops lay wilting from thirst. People were anxious and irritable as they searched the sky for any relief. Days turned into arid weeks. No rain came.

The ministers of the local churches called for an hour of prayer on the town square the following Saturday. They requested that everyone bring an object of faith for inspiration.

At high noon on the appointed Saturday the townspeople turned out en masse, filling the square with anxious faces and hopeful hearts. The ministers were touched to see the variety of objects clutched in prayerful hands—holy books, crosses, rosaries.

When the hour ended, as if on magical command, a soft rain began to fall. Cheers swept the crowd as they held their treasured objects high in gratitude and praise. From the middle of the crowd one faith symbol seemed to overshadow all the others: A small nine-year-old child had brought an umbrella.

LAVERNE W. HALL

Baptist
Minister

I have a cousin who is a Baptist minister. When we were growing up, we only saw each other a couple of times a year. Now we see each other even less.

A few years ago, when I hadn't seen him for some time, I suddenly began thinking about him and his family. I just couldn't get them off my mind. And for some reason, I felt compelled to send him a check for $100. I thought about it for a few days and made more than one aborted trip to the post office. I finally mailed it with a letter saying I hoped I wasn't offending him, but I believed the Lord wanted me to do this.

A couple of weeks later I received a reply. My cousin said it never ceased to amaze him how God worked in his life. And now God had once again shown him, through us, that he would always meet our needs. My cousin said the only concern he had was that I had sent too much. All he had needed was $97.56.

Lalia Winsett

Sunday School Lessons

The Sunday school lesson for the day was about Noah's Ark, so the preschool teacher in our Kentucky church decided to get her small pupils involved by playing a game in which they identified animals.

"I'm going to describe something to you. Let's see if you can guess what it is. First: I'm furry with a bushy tail and I like to climb trees."

The children looked at her blankly.

"I also like to eat nuts, especially acorns."

No response. This wasn't going well at all!

"I'm usually brown or gray, but sometimes I can be black or red."

Desperate, the teacher turned to a perky four-year-old who was usually good about coming up with the answers. "Michelle, what do you think?"

Michelle looked hesitantly at her classmates and replied, "Well, I know the answer has to be Jesus—but it sure sounds like a squirrel to me!"

SUSAN WEBBER

My Mother's Hands

A few years ago, when my mother was visiting, she asked me to go shopping with her because she needed a new dress. I don't normally like to go shopping with other people, and I'm not a patient person, but we set off for the mall together nonetheless.

We visited nearly every store that carried ladies' dresses, and my mother tried on dress after dress, rejecting them all. As the day wore on, I grew weary and my mother grew frustrated.

Finally, at our last stop, my mother tried on a lovely blue three-piece dress. The blouse had a bow at the neck-line, and as I stood in the dressing room with her, I watched as she tried, with much difficulty, to tie the bow. Her hands were so badly crippled from arthritis that she couldn't do it. Immediately, my impatience gave way to an overwhelming wave of compassion for her. I turned away to try and hide the tears that welled up involuntarily. Regaining my composure, I turned back to tie the bow for her. The dress was beautiful, and she bought it. Our shopping trip was over, but the event was etched indelibly in my memory.

For the rest of the day, my mind kept returning to that moment in the dressing room and to the vision of my mother's hands trying to tie that bow. Those loving hands that had fed me, bathed me, dressed me, caressed and comforted me, and, most of all, prayed for me, were now touching me in a most remarkable manner.

Later in the evening, I went to my mother's room, took her hands in mine, kissed them and, much to her surprise, told her that to me they were the most beautiful hands in the world.

I'm so grateful that God let me see with new eyes what a precious, priceless gift a loving, self-sacrificing mother is. I can only pray that some day my hands, and my heart, will have

earned such a beauty of their own.

Bev Hulsizer

To every thing there is a season,

and a time for every purpose

under Heaven. A time to be

born, and a time to die....

A time to weep

and a time to laugh.

ECCLESIASTES 3:1-2,4 NIV

May the road rise to meet you,

May the wind be always

at your back,

The sun shine warm upon your face,

The rain fall soft upon your fields,

And until we meet again

May God hold you in the hollow

of his hand.

Author Unknown